Research

Reflections and Suggestions
for Teachers for Creating a Community of
Research in Waldorf Schools

by

Torin M. Finser, PhD

Printed with support from the Waldorf Curriculum Fund

Published by:
Waldorf Publications at the
Research Institute for Waldorf Education
38 Main Street
Chatham, NY 12037

Title: Research: *Reflections and Suggestions for Teachers
for Creating a Community of Research in Waldorf Schools*
Author: Torin M. Finser, PhD
Editor: David Mitchell
Layout: Ann Erwin
ISBN # 978-1-943582-06-8

© 1995 AWSNA Publications
Redesigned and reprinted 2016 by Waldorf Publications
Cover art: *Color Study with Concentric Circles* by Wassily Kandinsky, 1913; watercolor, gouache and crayon on paper; in the public domain.

Table of Contents

Introduction

Waldorf teachers the world over have questions about their work, about their children, lessons, materials, and the functioning of schools as social organizations. These questions are real; they come from participation in the living stream of education. But are these questions always heard?

In striving to meet the needs of children, teachers practice observation. They look at temperaments and learning styles, social interactions, handwriting, walking, speaking, drawing. These observations are often child-specific yet relate to the age group in general.

Many of the observations provoke insights that can be helpful to other teachers. Can we find ways to share these child centered observations beyond the faculty circle in one particular school?

Many Waldorf teachers become librarians. They collect poems, songs, stories, skits, circle activities, science experiments, readers, plays etc., until after some years a teacher may possess a veritable treasure trove of materials. Within a school, there is often considerable sharing. Yet can we do more as a Waldorf movement to share resources?

Then there are the gems, those primary resources developed by teachers with special creativity and insight. I am speaking about original work, the pedagogical stories, plays, activities, lessons that were created in a burst of enthusiasm in response to a particular challenge or classroom situation. How can we foster and expand this creativity?

By the very nature of their tasks, teachers follow a path of inquiry. Yet the focus often shifts from week to week and block to block depending upon immediate demands. There is a need to focus and organize our research efforts.

In order to begin working with some of the questions raised in the above paragraphs, this pamphlet will look at some of the obstacles common to classroom research, possible goals and methods, working with a question, organizing and sharing. One section will describe a possible collaborative model for teacher research, and the conclusion will consider the spiritual implications of re-searching.

This is not an exhaustive study on research. The aim is to stimulate inquiry, discussion, and the practice of research in Waldorf schools.

Perceptions of Obstacles to Teacher Research

In speaking with practicing teachers, three constraints are repeated again and again: time, resources, and support. Here are the voices of a few public school teachers concerning research:

> "Time, time, time—resources, resources…. Can we look at teachers as professionals? As researchers? Should we look at teacher-researchers differently than teachers, and invoke incentives to do research… money, perhaps, but also time, recognition, space to try new ideas… support?"

> "Teachers seem to need more free time for research and for renewal. I wish schools could recognize this and somehow provide periods of time for professional work…. Perhaps floating teachers would help."

"Consider the economic and political implications of such research. What (administrative) entities have a vested interest in squelching it?"

"Time, support, recognition of teachers as professionals and as people with expertise…. The daily stress and demands right now are too much. We can't add more to teachers' lives. We must be able to incorporate research into present teaching…. Less would lead to more, more opportunities for meaningful research."

"Please consider our current time and isolating constraints. How can we convince the wider voting communities and administrators that we need time and each other—for the benefit of the children?"

The nature of the challenge may vary depending on each school, but the general themes emerging from Waldorf and public school teachers are remarkably similar. Any effort to enhance teacher research will by necessity have to take into full account the obstacles they face.

But looking squarely at the challenges also provides an opportunity to re-conceive, re-design, and rethink traditional assumptions about research (see next chapter). Any research effort by practicing teachers needs to begin with an understanding of the following points:

1. A teacher's primary task is to teach. Any research has to enhance teaching—if it is to be meaningful to both the teacher and the children.

2. It would be naïve to postulate that research does not consume a commodity in short supply, namely time. So, rather than adding another layer of work onto the teacher's day, how can research actually enhance the quality of teaching and thus potentially save time

in the end? If one can describe a situation in which preparation is facilitated and relationships within the school strengthened through research, one might be able to justify allocating some precious time for research. But for practicing teachers, if research is to be sustained over time, the results need to be practical and visible.

3. Methods used in such research will need to be in harmony with the demands of the classroom and the school day. Thus my main objective in the chapter on methods will be to demonstrate just how many possibilities are available for valuable research. One does not need to spend hours in the library to arrive at findings that may enhance education in more than one classroom.

4. If these findings are to have value beyond the life and the classroom of one particular teacher, we will need to find ways of sharing information that go beyond the traditional route of scholarly publication. Teacher research is meant to be used.

5. The above points translate into a bias towards qualitative research, especially action research rather than traditional quantitative research.

As Glenda Bissex said when she gave a guest presentation during my course on educational research:

Quantitative research seeks to prove something; qualitative research seeks to learn something.[1]

Teacher research is all about learning.

Reinventing Research: New Concepts, New Approaches

As an experiment, I asked a group of people to call out words that come to mind when hearing the term "research." They brainstormed as follows: library, footnotes, readings, communication, scary, deadlines, interviews, dry, stressful, graphs, bibliographies, hypothesizing, notes, data, variables, control groups, stilted … to list but a few. Needless to say, I was surprised to hear that most of these words described traditional approaches to research. No wonder teachers have found little time for such work!

If research means to look again and again, to be open to the unknown in the search for new meaning, then perhaps we need to begin with a new characterization of "research" itself. Traditional research, by the way, is not really that open to the unexpected, since the hypothesis anticipates an answer, and the data collected is supposed to be solid enough to constitute proof. Yet if one does a survey of the history of scientific research, for instance, one quickly realizes how soon the conclusions of one year are submerged by the totally new discoveries of the next. Besides, in the case of teachers, proof is often less important than learning. As stated by David Hopkins,

> Teachers and researchers do not conceptualize teaching in the same way. They live in different intellectual worlds and so their meanings rarely connect.…
> [T]he usual form of educational research, the psycho-statistical or agricultural-botany paradigm, has severe limitations as a method of construing and making sense of classroom reality.[2]

Thus teachers need a different approach to research if it is to have practical value.

In redefining "research," we can begin by examining our goals. For teachers, these might include:

1) Rather than serving as a means of gathering information, research for teachers can be a vehicle for gaining understanding.[3] This means formulating one's own questions, selecting a method that works for one's particular situation, and being content with results that may not "change the world" but might very well change an aspect of one's own teaching. Research for understanding involves a search for meaning rather than proof.

2) Being prepared for the unexpected, which requires an open mind and heart, a willingness to be surprised. Rather than an emphasis on control, teacher research needs to be flexible and varied (see chapter on methods). I am convinced that this attitude of open-mindedness has spiritual and pedagogical value in itself, even if nothing else is accomplished in the research process.

3) These qualities of openness and flexibility do not negate the need for the discipline of inquiry. Once a question is identified and articulated, one goal is to follow its path with consistency and true discipleship. If it is one's own question that one is following, if one owns it, the systematic line of inquiry with be less onerous.

4) This leads to another goal: Teacher research must be driven by burning interest. If one is not interested enough in a question to live with it for many months, find another one. The initial question needs an element of passion in order to be a long term companion.

5) Since teachers spend most of their time in action, doing things in the classroom with children, teacher-

driven research needs to be action based. "Put simply, action research is the way groups of people organize the conditions under which they can learn from their own experience."[4]

Action research can involve four phases: planning, acting, observing and reflecting. Much of this can be done in the classroom while teaching.

6) A final goal of teacher research involves the word "commitment." Oh, how much is perpetrated in the name of this word! Yet, if research is to take hold in our schools, we need teachers who are committed to a path of inquiry. Given the constraints on time and energy, I suggest a research commitment to a small question, something that might seem insignificant at first. For instance, rather than take a theme such as "How do children respond to mathematics when taught through motion in grades 1–5?," the teacher might begin with something that has clear parameters: "Are children more attentive on Monday mornings if the day begins with math-movement activities?" Make a commitment to something that can be completed (provided the teacher plans on teaching Monday mornings). Above all, make sure that the question selected directly relates to the rest of your teaching life.

Why Do Research?

In the spring 1994 issue of *Teacher Research,* Karen Ernst describes her experiences creating a community of learning, a group of teacher researchers. Afterwards, she asked the teachers to review their work together. The participants felt that the project had affected their classroom work in the following ways:

Increased sense of professionalism; increased
support for their own work through participation in
a community of colleagues; support for changes in
what or how they teach; awareness and practice in
observation and reflection on their classrooms; sense of
empowerment to answer questions, challenge the status
quo; and suggestions for changes in teaching practice.[5]

This summary statement prompts a more detailed examination of the benefits of teacher research and why this activity should be pursued more vigorously.

The Performance Gap

A growing body of research suggests, first, there is often
incongruence between a teacher's publicly declared
philosophy or beliefs about education and how he or
she behaves in the classroom; second, there is often
incongruence between the teacher's declared goals and
objectives and the way in which the lesson is actually
taught; and third, there is often a discrepancy between
a teacher's perceptions or account of a lesson and the
perceptions or account of other participants (e.g., pupils
or observers) in the classroom (Vide, Elbaz, 1983). All
of these discrepancies reflect a gap between behavior
and intention and are a source for classroom research
problems.[6]

Thus this gap between what is and what could be becomes a rationale for collaborative research. One might say that the kind of research model proposed at the end of this pamphlet could help keep us honest. Research is a means of self-evaluation and professional feedback.

Professional Development

It follows that teacher-directed research is likely to enhance teaching practices as the participant engages in a process of questioning, observing, refining and reshaping attitudes and opinions. This process of personal growth and change can have a liberating effect on the profession as a whole.

In recent years, state governments have imposed a web of restrictions and controls on public schools and have occasionally even ventured into the domain of private education. The public in general seems to continually demand more accountability from teachers and clearly defined educational outcomes. How can teachers respond to these demands? One way is to emphasize more internal accountability, to establish standards and goals based on teacher-driven research findings, and not those of local politicians, thereby reclaiming freedom in culture and education. "By adopting a research stance, teachers are liberating themselves from the control position they so often find themselves in."[7]

Increased public scrutiny can thus become an opportunity to emphasize professionalism rather than arbitrary criteria (or the norms set by standardized tests and Goals 2000). Teachers can assert leadership in their profession by shouldering more responsibility for their actions and creating a dynamic, creative learning environment through research.

Teachers as Role Models

Children learn not only through what is presented but by how the teacher goes about his or her own process of learning. Someone who is eagerly pursuing a theme in research will provide a role model for the children even if the subject itself is not shared in the classroom. Teacher research feeds the children, for, as described at the end of this book, when a teacher's ego intensifies its work upon the lower members, this transformative activity can enhance the quality of all teacher/child interactions. Thus, rather than being a cold, cerebral activity, research can actually increase the intimacy of relationships.

Shared Values

In the citation that began this section, the teachers used the word "support" several times in a few lines. Usually one thinks of research as a lonely activity, something that might only increase a sense of alienation and separation from the rest of the world as one sits in the local library. Yet an action-research model could become just the opposite. If one works as a team within the faculty, engages in classroom research with the students as collaborators, and shares the results with colleagues on a regular basis, one can accentuate the school as a community of learners with shared goals. This process can be sustaining and deeply encouraging.

Observation

> The range of what we think and do
> Is limited by what we fail to notice,
> And because we fail to notice
> That we fail to notice,
> There is little we can do
> To change
> Until we notice
> How failing to notice
> Shapes our thoughts and deeds.[8]
> – R.D. Laing

As long as we focus only on what we expect to see, we are functionally blind. To quote Glenda Bissex again, "The world around us is a text, and we have stopped being able to read much of it. We listen to the weather report rather than looking at the sky."[9] Research can bring us out of the realm of weather reports and reconnect us with the sky, the primordial expanse of real learning through observation. All teachers rely on secondary materials, source books, curriculum guides, lessons from other teachers—but do we have enough primary sources? It would be very healthy for our schools as cultural institutions if we once dared to throw out all the accumulated materials from other people and had to teach from direct observation of our students' needs.

Any research question based on classroom/school life, no matter how limited in scope, has the potential of sharpening our skills in observation that could then apply to a wide range of other activities. For example, observing how the children learn on Monday mornings before and after circle time, though very specific, would heighten the teacher's awareness of student responses throughout the week. Teacher research is needed not only for the specific findings that may arise, but for the all-important byproducts, such as a change in teacher consciousness. Once one really observes, one cannot stop. Research through observation becomes a healthy habit.

As a side remark, I would like to draw a slender yet vital distinction between "observation" and "inference." As Ted Sizer states in *Horace's Compromise,* "Everyday experiences show how important this distinction is. SAT scores have gone up two points. Some then hypothesize that because SAT scores have gone up, high schools must be getting tougher. The first statement is an observation, and the second a conclusion (of substantial dubiousness) drawn from the observation. Sloppy people confuse the two."[10] I would like to also recommend rereading chapter nine of *Study of Man* in regard to conclusions, judgments and concepts.

Social Change

Any meaningful teacher research has the potential to effect social change. One has only to read Paulo Freire's *Pedagogy of the Oppressed* (1972) to experience a vivid, anguished example of how educational emancipation goes hand in hand with social and political change. I can imagine a path of social/political emancipation as follows:

Teacher research as intense professional/spiritual striving
can lead to

An enhanced professional "voice" for teachers,
which can lead to

Strong, vibrant schools that serve as cultural centers,
which can lead to

Freedom for education and necessary restrictions on political and economic intrusionson cultural endeavors in general,
which may result in a

Reconfiguration of the social organism.

Teacher research is needed.

Seeing, Feeling, Finding Your Question

We all ask questions, of ourselves and others, all the time. These questions are varied and often not even verbalized. Some of our questions are factual in nature and are answered immediately: "Do I turn left on Hickory Street? How much does this watermelon cost?" etc. Other questions stay with us for a while: "How come, whenever I sit down to do some work at my desk, the phone always rings?" There are also questions that become companions, questions that remain with us for an extended period of time. It is these that are the focus of discussion in this section.

Traditional research suggests that you begin with a problem. If this is hard to identify, you might start a few sentences with the following phrases:

> I would like to improve the…
> Some people are unhappy about…
> What can I do to change the situation…?
> I am perplexed by…[11]

My preference is to find a question rather than a problem, and to do a series of "wonderings" to identify yours: "I wonder how… I wonder about… I wonder if…" You might make a long list in a stream-of-consciousness manner, then go back and find groupings: those that involve your class, the material, relationships, etc. When you have found your family of questions, try to formulate one question that speaks to the core issue.

Then try out your question on others. When I recently taught a workshop on educational research in Ann Arbor, I asked participants to write their question at the top of a blank page and pass it to the person on the left. We each had to react to the question in front of us. Some of the responses were along these lines: What do you really mean? This is not clear. Alternative phrasing could be. … Have you considered…? This is really three issues…. You might call so and so…, etc. Then we passed the pages to the next person, and so our questions made the rounds, receiving in all twenty-two responses. When our own questions had been returned to us after this round robin exercise, I asked that the feedback be considered overnight before we had small group meetings and individuals wrote up formal proposals for research. Most of the students in the class felt that this exercise was extremely helpful in terms of clarifying their thinking and that it also served as a validation of their issues and personal needs.

It is even possible to begin the research process without a clearly defined question. Here is another pearl from Glenda Bissex:

> One thing that I've learned from myself as an observer
> is how I can unearth or excavate my own questions
> by following my own observations. What attracts my
> attention as I observe and what I find myself recording
> is information to help me answer questions that I may
> not yet have consciously asked.[12]

Thus the process of finding a question and learning from it is a spiritual process that will be considered again in the last section of this pamphlet.

Jon Wanger speaks of how research can be designed to fill in blank spots in terms of questions already formulated and when one simply needs more information; or research can provoke new questions that illuminate blind spots in existing theories, methods and perceptions.[13] Both avenues help us see the phenomena before us more clearly than before.

Harry Wolcott is attracted to the idea "of thinking about research as problem setting, rather than problem solving."[14]

This consideration is helpful because teacher researchers might inadvertently set themselves up for failure if they expect to solve all their "problems" through research. It is important to remember that success and failure can be judged only in relation to what you set out to do (therefore don't bite off more than you can chew!), and that finding questions, formulating problems and key issues is in itself a worthy result of research. As with the Grail Mystery and the story of Parcifal, the Waldorf seeker might be content to plead: May I be so "present" that, if nothing else, I learn to ask the right questions!

This does not rule out the possibility for more traditional research if a teacher is so inclined. The above paragraphs describe a more open system in which the teacher engages in an activity that provides an issue and the basis for action research. Yet if one wishes to follow a more closed system, one can also formulate a hypothesis and engage in research that will supply data to support the theory. With this latter approach, and indeed with all research, it is particularly important to find the appropriate methods.

Some Thoughts on Research Methods

Before delving into specific suggestions on methodology, I would like to share a few reflections in a general way. The most significant discovery I made in my own research efforts was that so much can be discovered by using what is already at hand. One does not need to get on the plane, send away for all sorts of material, or run up a large phone bill in doing research. It is best to start with that which is readily available: the classroom, colleagues, parents, and the students' work and an ERIC search at the local library. It is possible that one might even save that plane ticket for the "last round" of the research, when one is thoroughly familiar with the subject and can make best use of an exotic visit. To modify a popular bumper sticker, research locally, think globally.

Also, it is important to sound another theme at this early stage: Consider those who are being researched. It is part of the abstract, (some might say) masculine tradition in research to delve in, collect the data one wants, and not consider the process from the point of view of those who are being observed. I suggest that at each stage and with each method, consider "how it feels" from the other end, and try whenever possible, to use non-intrusive methods of data collection. For example, instead of bringing in a video camera to observe social interactions (especially intrusive in a Waldorf classroom), try looking at carpet wear, listening to the children's comments, even examining the trash basket at the end of the day. Also, in an interview, it is not just the teacher who will be learning. Prepare a few questions, but leave time for those that may arise from the person being interviewed. The interview should really be a conversation. As one advisor in my doctoral program said, leave room for the unexpected in the interview conversation. Also record your contributions in the discussion, for you may say something in the context of the interview and the particular person that would not have been possible had you stuck to a straight question/answer format; in other words, you might discover something through the act of speaking.

Finally, by way of introductory comments, use triangulation. The suspicion concerning qualitative research has often been that it will be "soft" and unreliable. This makes triangulation all the more significant in terms of your credibility. Briefly put, triangulation means using three or more means to answer the same question. Thus if you want to find out what children have for breakfast,

1. ask them,
2. interview their parents,
3. send home a questionnaire to be completed over 5 days,
4. and, at a class night, ask the parents to go over the results with you.

The fourth step is one of my favorites. It again takes research out of the "superior PhD realm" and makes it a community event. You do not really know all the facts, yet after collecting some data, you are open to reviewing it with those who gave their time to help you. It also serves as a convenient way to correct misimpressions and possible bias on the part of the researcher. In real life, research is not a matter of data entry, but really a "spiraling in" toward greater understanding. Take your participants along on the journey!

What follows is not a list of methods to use, but rather an array of possibilities. Some may be more suitable for one given project than another. The element of freedom arises when one overcomes one's natural inclinations and tries a variety of techniques.

1) Be **Awake in the Moment.** As stated above, use the classroom. Examine your daily routine, the lesson, the human interactions in the light of your question. There is much that can be found in the ordinary.

2) **Field Notes.** Buy yourself a new binder with loose-leaf pages. Keep it on your desk in the classroom. In the morning, before the children arrive, reformulate your question at the top of the page and enter the date. Then during the day, make short entries; incomplete sentences are fine for this exercise. Then at the end of the day, make additions that were not possible while in the middle of things. Use descriptions, and do not

worry if things do not agree with each other. This method of taking field notes helps focus you on the issue over a period of time and is good for general impressions and descriptions that can be interpreted later.

3) **Audio Tape Recording.** Most Waldorf teachers discourage the use of electronic devices in the classroom, and for good reason. Yet there are ways to work with tape recording that I have found invaluable and should at least be considered in certain circumstances. A small tape recorder (I have one the size of my appointment book) can be kept in a desk drawer, or between two books. It can be turned on without any noise, used for brief periods, and then erased after listening to it in the evening. It is particularly useful for one-on-one interactions, less helpful when there is a lot of background classroom activity. If nothing else, a tape, done occasionally, can supplement other methods and help us listen with greater accuracy.

4) **Video Tape Recording.** This method is used increasingly in public schools and even in traditional teacher education programs. It is certainly intrusive, and I would not use it with young children (same with some of the constant photo taking at some of our assemblies and class plays!). Yet if working with older students, colleagues, parents or a community event, this method might be helpful in one's research, as one can view the interview or interaction again and again. Also, when one sees oneself in the video, it can promote a re-examination of gesture, movement and interpersonal interactions.

5) **Pupil Diaries.** In many schools, students are asked to keep a journal or daily log at one grade level or another. This practice can double for teacher research, in that one's assignment to them might include an

aspect that one is investigating. Since you would be checking their work anyway, this method of teacher research is highly time-efficient. Likewise, the student journal entries provide a stimulating counterpart to one's own field notebook (#2 above).

6) **Questionnaires.** More appropriate for older students and adults, this method allows you to ask very specific questions of a large number of people. The information can be collated by someone other than yourself if you are pressed for time, especially if you have used a scale, such as "often," "seldom," "never." For open ended questions, I suggest you read each one yourself, for often things are said "between the lines." One tip: Do a trial run first and then rewrite your questions. It is amazing how many ways a simple question can be understood. You want feedback from a few people so as to make your mistakes on a small scale before distributing the questionnaire to the masses. Also, it is not just the responses to specific questions that are of interest to the researcher, but the correlation of responses. You might even formulate the same question in different ways at various points in the survey.

A questionnaire allows you to cast a broad net and involve many people in your work. I advise my Antioch students to use this method early on in a research project, as it also helps identify issues and people for subsequent stages.

7) **Case Studies.** "A case study is individual research in a small context. We don't know enough based on our individual classroom case studies to know which are the generalizations that will hold true for other teachers. But other teachers will know! As teacher-researchers, we can't make those generalizations, but they will be made by our readers. I believe our classroom case

studies can offer valuable insights for other teachers, but the basis for those insights is not generalizations, but universals, which is also what makes literature endure. The things we have in common as human beings—those fundamental things that we have in common as teachers—are going to be there, in those case studies or pieces of literature. They endure because they continue to speak to what is fundamental in human experience, or in teaching experience."[15]

I found in my research that case studies were like writing a biography. I really got to know the people I worked with! After using some of the above mentioned methods, it was also refreshing to go into depth and explore issues with someone over time. We need longitudinal studies from Waldorf teachers who work with children for 8-12 years! The case study informs and complements the material gathered by other means.

8) **Documentary Evidence.** This sounds like the work of a detective, but it is actually one of the most readily available methods for Waldorf teachers. Our students create a wealth of material: main lesson books, compositions, drawings, paintings, homework assignments, projects, etc. All this becomes fodder for the researcher—if the eye is trained to observe. This means not just living in the moment with the child as the work is created, but afterwards stepping back and *seeing it again* with the eye of a researcher.

If nothing else, write your research question in big letters and stand it up on your desk. Then take a pile of the children's creations and look at each one in light of your inquiry. You will be amazed at what can be found!

9) **Peer Observation.** We often do not visit each other's classrooms enough. One way to build community in the school, share resources and do

research is to schedule a series of peer visits. Give your visitor a 5x8 note card with your questions or issues, and ask him or her to observe your lesson with these in mind. Be sure to have the follow-up conversation. Much may have been observed that you missed. Take notes during the dialogue. Write them up and a few days later share them with the colleague that visited. Again, this kind of research method helps create a circle of care.

10) **Critical Incidence Research.** We all know about those unexpected "happenings" that occur from time to time in schools. Use them. Take a series of incidents in one class over time and look at them. How did you respond? What was revealed? The critical incident is like a moment of wakefulness that can shed light on the larger picture.

11) **Interviews.** Already mentioned above, I would simply like to add that, in addition to the interviews you might conduct, there are third-party interviews that you may not have considered: classroom observer/student, student/student, observer/observer. You can facilitate the gathering of data without always being at the center of the action.

12) **Other methods** might include sociometry, slide/tape photography, clinical supervision, highly structured observation by an outsider, checklists, coding scales and much more. The best methods often arise when you are frustrated in using someone else's and you have to invent your own. Just be sure that you can clearly articulate what you are doing—and keep accurate records.

Educational research should include a literature review. What has been published on your theme? My students at Antioch have found the ERIC search in the computer lab invaluable. Even if you only scan much of the material, you need to know what others have done.

Finally, I need to say a few words about human subjects testing. Each professional field has its own guidelines, and it is *essential* that researchers follow these guidelines. Any intervention that can affect the subjects being investigated must be scrutinized from this perspective. For instance, when I did my case studies, I asked the teachers involved to sign a consent form in which, among other things, I promised not to release the information gathered to employers, to omit names if quotes are used, and in general, to do everything possible to respect the rights of those participating. In school situations, one may have to obtain parental consent for certain kinds of research. It is best to consult these professional guidelines *ahead of time.*

For those who want to read a much more comprehensive study on qualitative research, and can afford $44.95, I suggest *Qualitative Evaluation and Research Methods* by Michael Quinn Patton.

Organization

Imagine being outrageously successful with all of the above work. You now have a burning question (or two), lots of material has been collected through the use of documents, interviews, observations, case studies, etc., and now everything is heaped up on your table at home in one fascinating, but chaotic pile. There are many, when faced with this spectacle, who abandon the whole process at this point! As with the round "Sir Plus" in our first grade classrooms, it is far easier to amass a fortune than to organize, let alone analyze the material. Yet, it is essential for the research process that one go beyond collection to comprehension.

Organizing the material involves the exertion of the ego, and it is the first stage of analysis.

I suggest you begin by outlining some broad categories within your theme. Separate your material accordingly. You may well change your categories after a while, but in the initial sorting you are also beginning to "mix and match" information that will create new insights. Be sure to go through all the data.

Then you arrive at the weeding phase. Harry Wolcott has a good way of describing this:

> The critical task in qualitative research is not to accumulate all the data you can, but to "can" (i.e., get rid of) most of the data you accumulate. This requires constant winnowing. The trick is to discover essences and then to reveal those essences with sufficient context, yet not become mired trying to include everything that might possibly be described. Audiotapes, videotapes, and now computer capabilities entreat us to do just the opposite; they have gargantuan appetites and stomachs. Because we can accommodate ever-increasing quantities of data—mountains of it—we have to be careful not to get buried by avalanches of our own making.[16]

Of course, the ready availability of copy machines has not helped!

In organizing as with preparation for teaching, it is not how much material you have but rather how well you have worked it through. This sifting and sorting helps to connect you with the essentials. A few practical suggestions:

> 1) Use index cards or computer files, with the title of a category at the top of each section. You can move the cards or files around as need arises, but having the headings in front of you will help keep things organized.

> 2) In terms of facts, figures and especially citations, get them right the first time. As I found when editing

School as a Journey, one inaccurate or missing page number in the footnotes can take hours to rectify. Keep accurate records.

3) If you are going to write up your findings, decide early on if you will use the *Chicago Manual of Style* for your field or the APA standards. This can save a lot of time later on.

4) Keep a pencil and small notebook on you at all times. Even after the formal gathering of data is over (actually, it is never over; you just have to decide when to stop), you can have sudden inspirations or ideas that need to be noted down. Take advantage of the higher levels of cognition described in the last chapter— they are the gifts of the gods! (Even long meetings are remarkably productive in birthing inspirational thoughts!) Keep your notebook by your side.

Sharing Research

If the kind of action research described in the foregoing pages is to have legitimacy within the larger circles of our profession, it needs to be shared. This not only means the articulation of what we have discovered, but the feedback and consequent corrective measures that are needed.

Although we may never feel we know enough on a given subject to share the results of our research, we do know something, and even that needs the enhancement of feedback. Sharing puts one in a vulnerable position; there are risks involved. Yet the social and intellectual benefits are great. One basic way to begin is to write.

In a marvelous article that appeared in *Handbook of Qualitative Research* (Norman and Lincoln, 1994), Laurel

Richardson states, "I consider writing as a *method of inquiry*, a way of finding out about yourself and your topic…. Writing is also a way of "knowing"—a method of discovery and analysis. By writing in different ways, we discover new aspects of our topic and our relationship to it."[17] Thus writing is continued research, only on a different level. One is able to enter the imaginative realm as one becomes the creator of images.

I suggest you begin with a one-paragraph statement of purpose. If you cannot say the gist of your piece in one terse paragraph, it will certainly be harder to write a book. A statement of purpose can be as simple as the articulation of the issue or question studied, why you took it up, and the results. Remember, in this whole endeavor, you are not trying to prove or define anything.

Just describe and characterize (please reread chapter nine of *Study of Man*). Sometimes I advise students to pick up the phone and call a good friend. When the inevitable question arises, "So, what have you been doing lately?," just turn on a tape recorder and say something about your research, why you took it up, the bottom line, the findings. Then after the rest of the phone conversation is over, replay the section on your research and write it down. It will need some editing, but most likely you have the gist of a statement of purpose.

My emphasis on this first stage comes from experience in reading student research reports and masters projects. If the first part, the purpose, is not in focus, everything else becomes much more difficult. There is a special kind of soul economy in spending the time chiseling a clear statement to describe what the project is all about.

Then it is a natural next step to do an outline or sequence. Again, if past experiences with this sort of thing are intimidating, think of it as a table of contents. What are the main topics? In what order should they appear? Think about ways in which you can connect people with your work. What would interest your colleagues, parents?

A solid outline can mark the start of some serious writing. However, in my experience, things have never been as linear as they seem on this page. I have found myself writing snippets even as the research progressed, and therefore the actual outline changes as one releases the creative stream of the narrative. The basic elements described here are important, but the actual experience, at least for me, is of unexpected simultaneity.

Along with math phobia, writer's block ranks high on many people's most dreaded list. In large part, this is because writing is placed on such a high pedestal. It seems that many people subconsciously feel that if their work is not a bestseller they have failed as writers. Here you need to remember the words from Laurel Richardson cited above. If writing is part of the process of discovery, you might lower your sights, practice some humility, and just aim to understand the material collected in a new way. Start the writing as a *reflection* on your findings. Begin in a conversational manner, just talking about your research. Use the pen or computer to do the talking. Don't worry about paragraphs or anything remotely close to proper grammar. Just say something about your work.

Harry Wolcott adds, "Writing is a form of thinking. Writers who indulge themselves by waiting until their thoughts are 'clear' run the risk of never starting at all."[18] Put something down on your screen/paper. Then, if you are using word processing, it is so easy to make deletions, cut and paste, and correct mistakes. Before the computer, doctoral candidates took twice as long to complete their studies. (But can we use this "new free time" to best advantage?)

In addition to technical assistance, the process of writing is enhanced by a certain amount of self knowledge. Are you a morning or evening person? Do you need a stiff cup of coffee to get going, or a brisk walk? Know what works for you—and use it. For me, the early morning is writing time. Starting in early May, I used to rise early and do one narrative, class teacher report per day. After school was out, it was just a matter of making corrections and copying—a sufficiently onerous project in those warm June days!

Another suggestion: Think about the point at which you will quit each session, and how to take up the writing again later. Rather than stop at the end of a topic or section, I often found it best to stop just before the logical resting place, just before the end of a chapter. This meant that at the next session, I was forced to reread the previous section, do some editing, and then jump back into the stream of things without having to pull everything up from scratch. Again, the important thing is knowing what works for you.

Another statement of the obvious: The shorter the piece the more likely the possibility it will find readers. Qualitative research is meant to be read and used. If you can say it in a few words, do so.

Finally, at some point in this "will" exercise, you need to inform the readers about the nature and extent of your data base, how you collected the material, the methods used. They need to know how you went about your work, since the process influences the results. Again, when I read student reports, I usually turn first to the annotated bibliography. That tells me about the process and enlightens my reading of the text.

A Collaborative Model for Teacher Research

Looking at the larger picture of teacher stress and renewal, as I did during my doctoral research, I found that caregivers (nurses, parents, teachers) also need nurturing. To give without replenishment is to limit one's capacity to continue. How can one find the resources for personal and professional renewal?

I found that many teachers, despite participating in numerous meetings, often felt a high degree of isolation. Not only do our tasks limit the time we can converse together on a personal level, but the level of expectations is such that many feel inadequate, whether it be in drawing, singing, math or speech. It is hard to reach out from a position of vulnerability and ask for support. (Often, just as one is about to, a crisis comes along, we go back to the "day-to-day" survival mentality, and the armor of invincibility goes back on.) How can we better share our striving as human beings?

Collaborative research is an attempt to address these and other school issues. Collaboration means to work together, doing what any single one of us could not do alone.

If one really means this, then collaboration is not just a matter of sharing "results," but must characterize *each stage* of the research process. How can one be realistic, given the limitations of time and resources, and yet do research together? Is it possible to envision a model that is simple and yet multifaceted, one that does not take too much organizing and yet addresses other social and spiritual issues in the lives of teachers?

One first clue comes from the traditions of oral history. Describing a collective project of residents of Hackney in East London, Thompson (1978) reports the interviews of community members and their lives with the intent of giving "back to people their own history, on the one hand, to build up through a series of individual accounts a composite history of life and work in Hackney, and, on the other, to give people confidence in their own memories of the past, their ability to contribute to the writing of history—confidence, in their own words: in short, in themselves."[19]

This project involving the creation of an oral history reminded me that adults learn best from each other and through sharing experiences. This helped me formulate the following model for collaborative research:

A. Hearing Questions.

I suggest that at an early faculty meeting in the fall, a substantial portion of the afternoon be devoted to the sharing of questions as described earlier in this text. One might begin by asking that each teacher take ten minutes to quietly write down her/his "wonderings." Then I would divide the faculty into groups of three to share. The two members of each group that are listening would see themselves as coaches, first asking the colleague what kind of feedback would help, then perhaps asking questions for clarification, helping find connections between the wonderings, and in general, encourage. Then the roles in the small group would switch. At the end of the small group sessions, each teacher should affirm the feedback received and choose one question that is of greatest importance. This coaching stage needs at least an hour. Then the faculty could reconvene, and the chair needs to set the tone with a few words about their "circle of trust" and the spirit in which questions are shared. This might make it possible for each teacher to share a question that could serve as a companion for the school year, a question that has enough passion to enthuse commitment.

B. Finding a Structure for Questions.

Much time can be saved if the research process is looked at from the viewpoint of methodology at this early point. I suggest that AWSNA provide a research consultant to visit the school that has undertaken this project, to meet with colleagues individually to draw up an outline of how, when and where the research will be conducted. Some things could be demonstrated in a large group setting such as the faculty meeting, but other issues are really individual, and the methods used in research must suit the particular question. By having, say, the same consultant visit several schools, he or she could help teachers from different schools connect based upon shared interests. This research web would gradually provide a new layer of association.

C. Following a Question.

This stage involves data collection, as described above. I suggest that the faculty again find small groups to serve as a monthly check-in, at which time each member would expect to hear an update on progress to date. The importance here is not approval or even feedback, but rather staying with the task and reporting on progress. Support listening is crucial. This process is very much a part of learning. As stated by Jon Wagner, "Research itself is a form of learning, and research reporting a form of teaching."[20]

D. Collegial Review.

About half way through the year, each teacher could write a brief, three- to five-page narrative, describing the project—a sort of overview. This narrative would be shared in the cohort group of three and sent to the research consultant for review. This collegial review, if handled rightly, can be tremendously affirming, lessen the stress issues around research, and enhance the social life within a school through shared interests.

E. The Symposium.

I envision that in the spring there could be a festive symposium, in which 3–4 schools could hold a weekend conference to share some of their research projects. I suggest that the host school not be one that has done the collaborative research, so that the presenters are free to focus on their sharing. Each school should send the topics proposed for the conference to the AWSNA consultant, who would group them thematically. Also, some teachers might need to be dissuaded or encouraged. The consultant could also serve as the convener at the weekend conference, setting the tone for presentations to follow.

I suggest that each presentation be no more than 20–30 minutes, the distilled essence of a year's work! The inner activity in this process of winnowing can be rewarding for the presenter and will help keep the audience focused. One might have three to four such presentations around a common theme, preceded by speech or singing. After each cluster, I suggest a short break and then discussion groups that would look at themes arising from the reports and provide a vehicle for questions to the presenters (and thus the recapitulation of the entire process that began with questions!). One might have one group of presentations on Friday evening, one each on Saturday morning, Saturday afternoon and Sunday morning. The conference could end with a plenum on the research process, thus allowing for the rewrite of this booklet!

This symposium format, with the feedback mechanism built into the structure, also allows for a response to the Heisenberg Effect—the uncertainty principle that might cause some to question the accuracy of any study since the observer/researcher himself may have affected the results by his very presence in the equation.[21] One of the best ways to check up on ourselves and our biases is to share the results with the informants (those who participated) and our colleagues. Teachers know when something rings true or needs modification. Our colleagues are our best recourse in dealing with the uncertainty principle!

Please note what is not included in the above: antiseptic methods, a long research paper, onerous deadlines, and lots of extracurricular activities. Teachers already do much of what has been described. They go to conferences, read, meet, share, etc. This collaborative model is mainly an intensification of teacher preparation, with an eye towards forming a research community.

If possible, the proceedings of the symposium should be recorded, a transcript made, edited and then made available to teachers in other regions of North America. Over time, with alternating regions taking this up, a considerable body of primary material would become available to the Waldorf movement. Even before then, however, the social/transformative benefits would be felt in our schools.

Why Do Research Revisited: Spiritual Development

In this section I would like to just touch on a few themes and indicate areas that might prove fruitful to those looking at the research process as a matter of self development.

Here are a few themes:

Research as a Path of Knowledge

How can I learn what I need to know in order to teach?

This question is a constant companion to many a teacher.

Learning and teaching walk side by side down the path of life; the one is inseparable from the other. Learning through preparation and learning through teaching inform one another; they create the rich tapestry we call experience.

The demands of the profession are such, however, that many teachers move from one four-course meal to another; they learn the content needed in the immediate situation, but often have little time to process the experiences. Even though the content worked with may be rich, the preparation methods all too often consist of academic habits carried over from the teacher's own undergraduate years.

How can teachers renew the art of learning? One approach is to re-examine the process of knowing, to re-search.

In the booklet *The Stages of Higher Knowledge*, Rudolf Steiner describes four phases or steps in the path of knowledge:

> 1) Material Knowledge
> 2) Imaginative Knowledge
> 3) Inspirational Knowledge
> 4) Intuitive Knowledge[22]

I would like to use this sequence to indicate how research can enhance spiritual development and intensify the process of teacher preparation.

In the course of a day, we take in many sense impressions. These impressions come from objects and things around us in everyday life. Yet these sensations are meaningless without a response. We respond to the impression with our feelings, a part of our supersensible organism called the sentient soul. In the meeting of outer sensation and soul response, consciousness is born. One can then turn away from the original sense impression and, because of the inner activity involved in the response, an image remains. We can then "make sense" of the image by forming a "concept" out of the original image. For example, one might see a clipper ship in the harbor on July 4th, retain the image even when one turns away, and it is only when one forms the concept "ship" that one has achieved understanding. But a fourth element enters the process of material cognition, namely the organizing element of the ego. Through its activity, images and concepts are united and form the basis of memory. The image itself remains only as long as the soul is engaged in the sensory experience, but thanks to the ego, we are able to relate the impressions of today with those of the past; we are able to remember. This is the foundation of our inner life.

Also in regard to concepts, the ego engages in relational activity. It combines concepts, builds understanding, and through marvelous inner activity, helps the human being form judgments.

Thus material cognition is based upon the ability to process sensations so that an image is formed, a concept arises and is unified by the activity of the ego. Thus the act of cognition is the basic building block of research.

At the next, higher level of cognition, the sensation from without is replaced by an image from within. This is called *imagination*. Through this faculty, images can become active for the individual that are not dependent upon physical sensation, but can be nevertheless just as vivid and true. Through meditation and other exercises indicated in *How to Attain Knowledge of Higher Worlds*, the student is able to gradually learn to form meaningful images free of sensory stimulation. Yet the process of forming concepts and the relatedness achieved by the ego remain just as important, if not more so, than before, in that one has to learn to discern real images from flights of fancy. When working with imaginative cognition, the responsibility of the researcher becomes all the greater.

In the third stage, image no longer plays a role, for now one is working just with "concept" and "ego." The human being lives wholly within the spiritual world. The stimulation of sensation in the first stage is replaced by *imagination* in the second and *inspiration* in the third stage of cognition. One is able to truly hear the tones of the spiritual world, one is able to penetrate to the very heart of things.

And finally, in the fourth stage, the ego remains alone. The experience, as related by Rudolf Steiner, is that of no longer being outside of things and occurrences, but now one stands within them. What lives in the soul has become the object itself. This living into things is called *intuition.*

Although this booklet has dealt mainly with techniques on the first level of knowing, material cognition, it seemed essential to describe the full process available to the student of higher knowledge. For research and self development are, in my opinion, vitally connected. The results achieved at one level can only be fructified and enhanced by striving of another level of insight.

In working with the above passages, it occurred to me that those engaged in research have, especially in recent years, articulated numerous avenues of inquiry that somewhat parallel the four stages just described. For instance, heuristic research attempts to get inside of the experience, qualitative research accepts the role of intuition's getting to the essence of the question, phenomenology accepts the importance of both outer and inner events as in the second stage, and traditional, quantitative research places an emphasis on that which is linked to sense perceptions.

Depending upon the subject of the inquiry, those engaged in research are advised to consider not only the content but also the process that is most suitable. Do we want to look at things from the outside or from the inside? In everyday life, one usually experiences the world from outside and oneself from inside. Research contains the possibility, if necessary, of reversing this: to experience things as if from the inside and oneself as if from the outside. Knowledge of the world thus goes hand in hand with knowledge of self. And how we get there is just as important as what we find.

One also has to start somewhere. So often teachers shy away from even the thought of research, and thus I have tried to address research on a simple, "first steps" basis, in the hopes that some new activity is stimulated. Part of the challenge is simply organizing ourselves, learning how to ask the question, observe, collect and share. But I hope the process is both internal and external, that self development goes hand in hand with strengthening our association as schools. And on both fronts, may we be known for our original work!

Research as Teacher Empowerment

This is a natural result of the research process. As we intensify our observations, gain understanding as well as self knowledge, reflect on practice and learn to better articulate what we are doing, we can experience a new kind of professional and personal freedom. This can lead to new roles in educational leadership and community activism.

Research as Renewal.

Already mentioned earlier, one might simply take up the theme of stress transformation. Find something that bothers you and make it your research question! It is amazing what happens when a source of frustration is brought under observation and study for a period of time.

Research and Professional Development.
If we as teachers are actively engaged in learning through research, our students benefit immediately. Our involvement, even if not on grade-level material, acts as a quickening element in their learning. Our vitality and enthusiasm directly affect the etheric health of the children.

Research and Anthroposophy.
I strongly recommend that, when following the process of research described above, teachers adopt one basic book to live with for an entire year. These are particularly helpful to the teacher researcher:

> *Philosophy of Spiritual Activity*
> *Practical Training in Thought*
> *Knowledge of Higher Worlds*
> *Occult Science*

Just consider for a moment the value of the basic exercises in light of the research process: open-mindedness, positivity, control of thought, etc. I am personally convinced that teacher research can enhance our anthroposophical work and that personal engagement in anthroposophy can enhance research in more ways than I can as yet imagine.

This leads me to my final observation:

Research as a Deepening of Waldorf Education.
On September 6th, 1919, at the end of his address, Rudolf Steiner called attention to something which he wanted to lay upon the hearts of the teachers present. These are principles of utmost importance:

The teacher must be a person of initiative in everything he or she does, great and small.

The teacher should be one who is interested in the being of the whole world and of humanity.

The teacher must be one who never makes a compromise in his or her heart and mind with what is untrue.

The teacher must never get stale or grow sour.[23]

If one lives with these four statements and the text that accompanies them, one cannot but see the relevance of teacher-inspired research.

Last year our Waldorf movement celebrated its 75th anniversary. Several schools on this continent have been in existence for over 50 years. Much has been accomplished. Although new schools are constantly beginning, I feel that as a school movement we left the pioneer stage some time ago and have, on the level of the Association at least, progressed far in terms of the organization stage. As with adult human development, we are now approaching the period when less is given to us as a free gift, so to speak, and more must be won through conscious effort. Rather than rely just on the treasures passed on by the early pioneers in Waldorf education, we need to take initiative, become authors in the larger sense. Research affords us an opportunity to accept the challenge of the age of the consciousness soul, pass through the eye of the needle, and come through our experiences as individuals who speak with a new voice. This next stage of our work is not a luxury; it is a necessity.

The creative forces that may be released from enchantment, if teacher research is truly taken up, cannot be fully imagined.

It all begins with the response of each individual to this call. Let me end with a passage from *Leaves of Grass* by Walt Whitman:

> You shall no longer take things at second or third hand,
>   nor look through the eyes of the dead, nor feed on
>   the spectres of books,
> You shall not look through my eyes either, nor take
>   things from me,
> You shall listen to all sides and filter them from
>   yourself.[24]

Appendix

In 1992, the Waldorf Teacher Education Program at Antioch New England launched an Experienced Educators Program, otherwise known as 3+2 (three summers and two additional semesters). From the beginning, research was an integral part of the first year, as the students selected themes to work with between the first and second summer sessions. The program accepted a second group of students in July 1994. After a year of "living with a question" and doing research as described in this book, they returned in July 1995, to take further courses and share their findings. I asked them to share reflections on the research process, some of which are included in this appendix.

"The research and deepening of one's work, in my case foreign language teaching, can ignite renewed forces from within which can manifest themselves as enthusiasm and interest in one's teaching and working with the children. Through a deeper esoteric understanding and research in one's field and as an anthroposophist, the knowledge gained through research brings one closer together with fellow Waldorf teachers in a common striving. In this way, we can support each other and nurture each other through sharing of our work and findings."

– Sandra Houston

"For me, the real heart of the process of research manifests itself in my everyday work with children. The in-depth reading can then find support to my on-going process as a teacher.

Life is a constant state of becoming. When we do not work with the principle of continuous growth, we lose an important dynamic in our work with children, and we also run the risk of materialization of the spirit (dogmatizing something that should be on-going process of maturation). Everyday is a new opportunity to learn from our work. What I discovered in my independent study research is that data gathered from a living process is a vital and valid way to sustain continuous research as a teacher.

"Sharing through a presentation or the writing of a paper then becomes one step along the way. The spring waters of evolving consciousness through teaching are ever flowing."
— Peggy Cooper

"My independent research which centered on the topic of child observation helped me to deepen my understanding of the child as she unfolds during each developmental stage and to look with *new* eyes in a comprehensive way at every child. Knowledge led to interest and interest to love, a love, I trust, that will guide me in my work with children."
— Barbara Bedingfield

"I had no idea how much I was to learn doing this research! What began as an idea to incorporate the *travel* experience (somehow) into the learning environment of the Waldorf high school student eventually turned into a study of the Luciferic and Ahrimanic forces at work in ancient Mayan ritual! And I got to bring twelve Waldorf high school students to the ancient sites in the Yucatan (for a two-week trip) to boot! You never know where (the process of) research will lead you. A *tiny idea* can turn into a *career*. We ask questions that only we could ask. We investigate because it has become so much a part of what we find we need to know.

And the process of *research* naturally translated into a real, confident understanding—*knowledge* that we can use and weave into our lives. I believe I learned quite a lot about not just the subject I'm researching—but about myself....

In our teaching, we can take what we've learned, of course, and apply it in the classroom. But just importantly—through our striving to understand our subject (via research)—we naturally reflect this striving to our children, giving them a quiet example to aspire to."   – Marc Harrington

"Doing research gives one an opportunity to delve into something with a depth that life seldom allows for in this day and age. It can be a counterpoint to balance the alacrity and shallowness of our other daily demands and pressures. To carry a question into waking and sleeping and through transformations of your own thinking is almost a form of meditation. To write it down is to allow others also to drink from the deep waters of your refreshing pool."   – Sandra Ruggiero

"The activity of engaging ourselves in individual research projects brings a real liveliness to the study of anthroposophy and Waldorf education. When a topic such as the wisdom of fairy tales is researched, put into practice, and shared among colleagues, it gains a strength that it didn't have before. The kernels of truth that have been lifted from the research on practical applications can be planted in other Waldorf classrooms and life situations. This idea of shared research is much like re-seeding the garden each year so that it will continue to flourish."

                                        – Janey Newton

"The activity of research serves two important functions: 1) As an exploration in more depth of questions and thoughts which seem important to our individual growth and inner purpose, and 2) as it results in a movement forward to communicate to others what stirs our deepest human interest. This process of articulation is essential to participating actively in the social realm."   – Steven Montgomery

"While I have long had a deep love and connection with the French language, my research enabled me to penetrate the genius of the language. With a better understanding of the development of the French language, I came upon the greater revelation of the evolution of human speech, speech in its highest glory and darkest hour."   – Emily Bowers

"Research is essential for the carpenter as well as for the teacher as well as for the philosopher. In order to work at the highest level possible, it is necessary to equip oneself with the best tools. But the question of research goes beyond the act of acquiring information. Life is a continual flow. In order to offer something—work, thoughts, whatever—to the world and to society, there must be an incoming flow to the doer, and this is research, whether of a factual or spiritual nature. It is food for humanity."   – Bethany Craig

"Researching my topic was an opportunity to step back and better understand the context the Waldorf schools occupy with regards to public education. By characterizing the public school approach to environmental education and science, I was able to go on to survey just what had been founded as an approach to nature in the Waldorf schools. The most important aspect of the research was the new insights which I was able to synthesize and develop from the wide range of literature which I surveyed. My ability to speak intelligently about the Waldorf approach has greatly improved, and I believe my opinions are authentically grounded now in my own efforts and understanding. I would recommend research as a discipline to anyone who would wish to usher Waldorf education into the next century."

– Gregory Albright

"As I mulled over this question, I realized that, as an avid reader and quester, I've been engaged in a lifelong research project. Yet, in my work of delving into the wisdom of fairy tales this past year, I noticed a real shift in lifestyle. Though I only scratched the surface of this rich topic, the changes came in my whole attitude. 'I'm doing research,' I often found myself reporting proudly to anyone who would listen. Being in this mode meant that I was able to digest and articulate the material in a living way.

"Knowing that my Antioch group-mates were similarly engaged was a great source of strength during the intense research period. I intend to take up a new research project (on the Sophia) in September. I'm interested in hearing more about collaborative research."   – Melissa McCall

"The idea of doing educational research sounded somewhat dreadful until the actual midpoint of my first project. By then I had done enough reading, interviewing and observing that exciting correlations were forming. Questions arose that I lived with as I continued looking into the literature and observing children. The actual paper-writing was a renewal and portal for future research. I learned that research creates faculties we may use for greater understanding of our children."

– Ann Sauer

"My anthroposophical research has a threefold quality to it: the reading, the writing and the presentation. I found the quiet inner activity of research complemented the busy outer activity of my days. Reading with a question, a focus, increased my depth and encouraged me to wrestle with the material. This had a vivifying effect on my life. The process of writing went beyond compilation: It was as if all that I had taken in nurtured a seed within me. In tending this seed, it gradually ripened until something new had grown in me. Writing out of this inner conclusion was exhilarating. I then entered the social realm with the presentation of the essence of my work. This inspired me to take my paper to a different level, an imaginative, audience-friendly one, which led me to new insights on my topic. I breathed in with the research and out with the presentation. The whole process greatly strengthened me physically, emotionally and mentally. I have a solid footing in one aspect of anthroposophy now and a matrix to which I can relate new information and insights. The spiral continues. The fruits multiply."
                                              – Kathleen Reagan

"Winter evenings reading and carrying images into sleep; trips to the library, telephone conversations, stints at the computer, beginning to write things down. Searching, looking and finding again. Research? Gathering scattered threads together, starting to weave. Just a small piece of cloth, but so satisfying! Fit one small piece to another small piece, the cloth grows. This work made a rich and private inner haven for me—the task of writing, bringing my thoughts and feelings to form; seeing the rich colors swirl into shape and solidify. This was both a discovery and an exercise of will. Finally, presenting my winter-work to a group of colleagues spread the whole cloth out, a blanket for our mental picnic. I experienced this task as a way

of connecting—with myself, with others and with the world that holds us all."
– Kate Gage

"To devote time that allows immersion into research is a gift to oneself. It is also a beginning in many ways. To begin with the whole of the universe and its mysteries, to take one idea from it, to develop and explore it, to find its connections to the whole—in this, we find understanding, growth and confidence. We feel more empowered by our understanding and realize that this can be a beginning, a way for us to see the world one piece at a time."
– Judith Selin

Endnotes

1   Glenda Bissex, from a guest appearance at Antioch New England, 1994

2   David Hopkins, *A Teacher's Guide to Classroom Research*, (Salisbury, UK: Open University Press, 1985), p. 29.

3   Ruth Shagoury Hubbard and Brenda Miller Power, *Teacher Research: The Journal of Classroom Inquiry* (Albany, NY: The Johnson Press, 1994, Vol. 1) p. 72.

4   Op. cit., Hopkins, p. 33.

5   Op. cit., Hubbard and Power, p. 67.

6   Op. cit., Hopkins, p. 48.

7   Ibid., p. 3.

8   Taken from syllabus used by Dr. Heidi Watts, a colleague at Antioch New England and an inspiration for this entire project.

9   Op. cit., Hubbard and Power, p. 79.

10 Theodore Sizer, *Horace's Compromise* (Boston: Houghton Mifflin Co., 1985), pp. 99–100.

11 Op. cit., Hopkins, p. 46.

12 Op. cit., Hubbard and Power, p. 75.

13 Jon Wagner, "Ignorance in Educational Research Or, How Can You *Not* Know That?" In *Educational Research*, Vol. 22, No. 5, pp. 15–23.

14 Harry F. Wolcott, *Writing Up Qualitative Research* (London: Sage Publications, 1990), p. 31.

15 Op. cit., Hubbard and Power, p. 82.

16 Op. cit., Wolcott, pp. 35–39.

17 Laurel Richardson, "Writing: A Method of Inquiry," in *Handbook of Qualitative Research*, Norman Denzin and Yvonna Lincoln, eds. (London: Sage Publications, 1994), p. 516.

18 Op. cit., Wolcott, p. 21.

19 Elliot G. Mishler, *Research Interviewing: Context and Narrative* (Harvard University Press, 1991), p. 15.

20 Op. cit., Wagner, p. 20.

21 Op. cit., Hubbard and Power, p. 74.

22 Rudolf Steiner, *The Stages of Higher Knowledge* (Hudson, New York: Anthroposophic Press, 1967) pp. 4–10.

23 Rudolf Steiner, *Towards the Deepening of Waldorf Education* (Forest Row, Sussex, UK: The Steiner Schools Fellowship Pub., 1977), pp. 26–27.

24 Walt Whitman, *Leaves of Grass* (New York: Signet Classic, New American Library, 1955), p. 50.